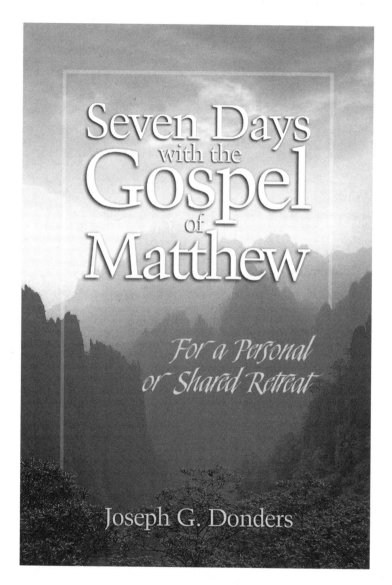

Seven Days
with the
Gospel
of
Matthew

*For a Personal
or Shared Retreat*

Joseph G. Donders

TWENTY
THIRD 23rd

Twenty-Third Publications
A Division of Bayard
One Montauk Avenue, Suite 200
New London, CT 06320
(860) 437-3012 or (800) 321-0411
www.23rdpublications.com

ISBN-10: 1-58595-549-3
ISBN 978-1-58595-549-7

Library of Congress Catalog Card Number: 2005934264
Printed in the U.S.A.

Seven Days with the Gospel of Matthew

For a Personal or Shared Retreat

CONTENTS

SUGGESTIONS FOR MAKING A RETREAT

Prepare a quiet place where you can make your retreat. Set up a few symbols that might help create a prayerful atmosphere, such as a statue, a cross, an icon, or a candle. Sit in a comfortable chair. Have a notebook ready to write down your thoughts, feelings, and ideas.

Set the time limit for your reflection; a half-hour to an hour per meditation might do. Use the morning meditation before you begin your day, and the evening meditation either at the end of your work day or before going to bed.

Avoid distractions; try to relax and empty your mind of all worries and concerns. Know that you are in God's presence, and that God is present in you, your family, your community and the world.

Read the Scripture passage cited at the beginning of each meditation. Allow the words to fill your mind. Pause at the words or phrases that speak to you in a particular way, that touch your mind or your relationships, and your life. The suggestions in the *For Reflection* section will help spark some ideas.

Try to listen to what the Spirit is saying to you. Remember that the most important part of prayer is to be attentive to God's word. Be open to that word, even when it challenges you to live as you have never lived before.

Begin a journal that you will use throughout the retreat; there are pages provided for this purpose starting on page 50. Record in it your thoughts and prayers, as well as the moments when you are most aware of God's presence in your life.

INTRODUCTION

Through the pages of this little book, I invite you to reflect on Matthew's gospel and use it to make a mini-retreat, a prayerful time away in the midst of your daily tasks and responsibilities. This may mean getting up earlier than usual for a morning meditation, and putting aside tasks earlier than usual for an evening meditation.

During this seven-day period we will focus together on the spiritual advice found in the gospel of Matthew. We will follow the developments in the discoveries made by the people who surrounded Jesus. Like the other gospels, the gospel by Matthew—some would call it the gospel "of"' Matthew—presents itself as one book with its own message. Though Matthew is the first of the gospels—in order—in the New Testament, it is not the oldest. Centuries ago Saint Augustine gave the Gospel of Matthew the place of honor. He considered Matthew's gospel to be the most complete, the most well-known and also the first one written. According to Augustine, Mark's gospel was just a short rewrite of Matthew's gospel.

Nowadays researchers are of a different opinion. They consider Mark's gospel to be the first and original one. They point out that Matthew uses about 600 verses of Mark's gospel. According to them Matthew must have been written around the 80s, after the destruction of Jerusalem and its temple by the Romans in the year 67. Mark's gospel, instead, was written years before that event, for the Christians persecuted in Rome.

The destruction of Jerusalem and especially of its temple had an enormous impact not only on the Jewish people who are still experiencing the effects but also on the young Judeo-Christian community. Those who survived the destruction had dispersed all over the Middle East. The devastation of the temple affected them not only physically and psychologically, but also spiritually.

These Christians had been eagerly awaiting Jesus' speedy return, as did Saint Paul when he wrote his first letters. Their expectation must have grown during the siege of Jerusalem, and they viewed the fall of

Jerusalem as the moment of Jesus' return as the Messiah who would restore and renew the world and establish the kingdom of God on earth. Nothing of the kind happened. The Christians must have felt disillusioned, discouraged, perhaps even bitter. Within this context Matthew, who according to most biblical scholars was a Jewish Christian himself, was inspired to study once again the teachings of Jesus. Moved by the Spirit he reinterpreted the good news of Jesus Christ.

Matthew seemed to refer to the pastoral need he felt impelled to address when he quoted Jesus' saying: "Every scribe who has been trained for the kingdom of heaven is like the master of the household who brings out of his treasure what is new and what is old" (13:52). He clearly indicated the intention of his gospel: to speak first of the new kingdom then the old!

It was not only the disappointment of the Jewish Christians that Matthew wanted to address. Times had changed. The people he wrote for were no longer the very poor, or the persecuted Christians in Rome whom Mark had addressed. In Mark's gospel Jesus tells his disciples to take "no copper coins" with them (6:8). In Matthew's version of the same event, Jesus tells them to take "no gold, or silver, or copper in your belt" (10:9).

Throughout his gospel Matthew refers to gold and silver more often than Mark and Luke combined. In Luke's version of the beatitudes Jesus simply blesses the "poor" (6:20). In Matthew's gospel, instead, he blesses "the poor in spirit" (5:3). Times had changed, indeed!

Other elements indicate that Matthew is addressing another class of people. In his gospel, the words "villages" and "villagers" are only mentioned four times, while the words "towns" and "townspeople" are mentioned about twenty-six times. Matthew wrote for middle-class people who were quite discouraged, without much hope, rather disparaged, and consequently without a clear sense of their mission in this world. They were—perhaps—not so very different from many of Jesus' followers in our own time.

Matthew's whole gospel attests to Jesus' mission to introduce a "new" world, a "counter" world, a world of righteousness, the reign of God. Entrusting the realization of this "newness" to his disciples, he gave them what one might call the "declaration" of this new kingdom in his Sermon on the Mount and in the eight Beatitudes, followed by a set of counsels on how to form this new community in handling conflict, taking oaths, sexual relations, the use of money, superfluous clothing, fraternal correction, dealing with one's enemies, and so on. All of this Jesus summarized in the answer he gave to a lawyer trying to test him: "You shall love the Lord your God with all your heart....This is the greatest and first commandment. And a second is like it: You shall love your neighbor as yourself" (22:37–39).

He told his disciples and us to share in his life and mission "You are the salt of the earth, you are the light of the world" (5:13–14). Breaking his bread and sharing his wine he shared with them his body, soul, life, and spirit (26:25–28), as he has done since with his followers all through the ages, as he does with us and as he will do until God's reign has been realized. He invites us again and again: Take this bread and drink this wine, until that day "when I drink it new with you in my Father's kingdom" (26:29).

As we make our retreat, we will reflect on some of the main points in the gospel of Matthew. In doing so, we pray that the words of Jesus may affect our lives today as they affected the lives of the persons he met long ago. May we come to a new understanding not only of the life of Jesus, but of our own lives, too.

FIRST DAY

M O R N I N G   M E D I T A T I O N

"Emmanuel, 'God is with us'"

Read Matthew 1:18–28

The first person we meet in Matthew's gospel is Joseph, Mary's fiancée. He notices that his future bride is pregnant. So the story seems to begin when after the annunciation Mary returned from her six months' visit to her cousin Elizabeth (cf Lk 1:39).

Joseph also knew that the child to be born was not his. Initially he must not have known how to react. He was a good, righteous, and loving person and did not want to expose Mary to disgrace and possibly even to death according to the laws of those days. So he decided to take the responsibility for the child upon himself, but to divorce Mary and not reveal the truth to anyone.

Just when he had resolved to do this an angel appeared to him in a dream to explain the situation. The angel informed Joseph that the child conceived in Mary was from the Holy Spirit, and told him not to be afraid to take Mary as his wife. Joseph therefore takes Mary as his wife and adopted her child as his own. The angel also told Joseph what name to give the child. He should be called Jesus—meaning "Yahweh saves"—because this child would save his people from their sins.

Another name was to be given to the child, one not mentioned in any other gospel: Emmanuel, meaning "God is with us." God was truly present with Mary and Joseph during the time Jesus was with them.

But that is not the whole story about the significance of that second name. Jesus' own final words at the end of Matthew's gospel are practically a repetition of that name, when Jesus assured his disciples, and consequently all of us, "And remember, I am with you always, to the end of the age" (28:20).

The whole Good News story as told by Matthew is summarized by those words at the beginning and end of his gospel: "God, Jesus, is with us," for all time. In Matthew's day that message had a special meaning. It responded to the state of affairs in the community Matthew addressed.

As noted in the introduction to this book the mainly Jewish or Judeo-Christian community Matthew addressed was a discouraged group of people. They had never really understood the mission Jesus had given them at his ascension, namely, to continue his mission. They must have been expecting him to return when the temple in Jerusalem was destroyed. He had not come. They were not only disillusioned; they had also lost most of their initial enthusiasm and hope.

They had been waiting for someone who had already come and who had been with them. They were waiting for the fulfillment of a task that had been commissioned to them!

Matthew tells us in his gospel the story of someone else who seems to have been disappointed in Jesus the Messiah. Perhaps he was not so much disappointed himself, but only trying to help his own disciples overcome their disappointment.

John the Baptizer, who was in prison at the time, sent some of his disciples to Jesus to ask him: "Are you the one who is to come, or are we to wait for another?" (11:2–3). Jesus replied that they should tell John not to be scandalized, that marvelous things were happening: the lame walked, the blind saw, the lepers were cleansed, the dead raised, and the poor had the good news brought to them. In other words the situation in the world was not going to change at one enormous blow, but things were happening, and the process was on its way.

Joseph and Mary experienced this in their own lives. They remained the victims of the common (and even worse) happenings going on around them. The angel would appear to Joseph again and again to tell him to escape to Egypt and then to return to Nazareth in Galilee and not to Judea as he intended to do. The angel brought him warning after warning, and Joseph and Mary had to pack, sack, and travel.

Jesus was with them, but his mother and foster father had to help themselves in everything they were asked to do. God's presence was intimately interwoven with their own lives in even the most common things. Jesus had to be fed, his diapers (or swaddling cloths) had to be changed; they had to help him begin to walk and speak.

Matthew stresses this presence of God in even the smallest things when he describes how Jesus would later say: "Have no fear... not even [the smallest sparrow] will fall to the ground unperceived by your Father. And even the hairs of your head are all counted. So do not be afraid; you are of more value than many sparrows" (10:29–31).

Joseph is an example of what it means to be engaged in the process of God's activity in this world. It is up to him to make decisions in the difficult moments of his life, even when guided by an angel. Likewise, it was Mary who had to face the complications in her life when she was contacted by an angel, asking her to be the mother of Jesus.

When they were asked to take part in Gods' redemptive initiative in this world, Joseph and Mary were faithful in their everyday life, an example to all of us who are engaged in the same process and mission.

FOR REFLECTION

- Why are you making this retreat? What do you hope to accomplish during this time?

- Do you relate the usual activities in your life to the task Jesus left to his disciples in the world?

- Do you experience Jesus' presence? When and how? Consider, for example, Matthew 18:20 and 28:16–20.

MORNING PRAYER

Loving God, be with me during these days of retreat in a special way.
Help me realize that in walking with Jesus
I share in his mission of restoring your reign in our world. Amen.

FAITH RESPONSE FOR TODAY

Take some moments of your time off today to reflect on how Saint Joseph's attitude in life might be an example to you.

EVENING MEDITATION

"His star at its rising"

Read Matthew 2:1–12

Suddenly some unexpected visitors interrupted the humdrum of Mary and Joseph's daily lives in Bethlehem. Another gospel tells us that the holy couple had already been visited by angels, and that the local shepherds with their sheep and dogs had come to see the mother and child. These new visitors, however, came from very far, from the East.

These wise men had already caused some consternation in the temple of Jerusalem and sown some panic at King Herod's court when they asked about the new king of the Jews, whose star they had seen rising in the sky. They had come, so they said, to pay him homage, bringing gifts of gold, frankincense, and myrrh.

Even if Matthew's story is not completely true but contains some elements of legend as opposed to only historical facts, as some commentators think, it is an important one. Matthew wanted to tell his readers about something they really should reflect on, something he had already hinted at when he began his gospel by outlining the genealogy of Jesus. He began the family tree of Jesus' foster father Joseph with Abraham, the first Jewish ancestor, but he had mentioned among Joseph's forebears four women.

Including women in a family tree was a very unusual practice in those days. Only forefathers, only men were usually named, which Matthew did in the rest of his genealogy. Even more remarkable is the fact that all four women mentioned are non-Jewish: Tamar, Rahab, Ruth, and a woman Matthew does not name but only refers to as the wife of Uriah, a Hittite; her name was Bathsheba.

Matthew made it clear that the Hebrew world had already been meeting and melding with the non-Gentile world. In a way this was already a sign of the fulfillment of the promise Yahweh once made to Abram and Sarai—as they were called when God addressed them for the first time. He told them that not only would they be blessed if they remained faithful to their call, but that in them, all the nations of the earth would be blessed (Gen 18:18).

The visit of the foreigners to Bethlehem should perhaps be seen as a further indication of the fulfillment of God's promise, the final peaceful gathering of all the nations on earth. Those wise men from the East traveled to greet the one who had come to gather the whole human family around the table of God the Father. In Matthew's gospel Jesus himself would later explicitly state that he had come to gather us together (12:30; 23:37). Anyone who reads the signs of the times in our day must realize that this message and the task of uniting people is one of the greatest challenges in our era of globalization, impending ecological disaster, interdependence, and religious and cultural strife.

Those wise visitors from the East were moved by their expectation of a restored world, of a redeemer, of someone who would lead them on the way to peace. At that time such an expectation was alive not only in the messianic expectations of the Jewish people but among many other people as well. We can even trace this expectation in the classical authors of those days, who were contemporaries of Matthew: Virgil, Tacitus, and Suetonius, for example.

This issue and message was of special importance to the readers Matthew addressed: the Jewish-Christian community dispersed all over the then-known world of the Middle East. Such a message was intended to help them widen their circle and welcome other people.

On the feast of Saint Francis of Assisi in October 1986, Pope John Paul II invited religious representatives from all over the globe to come to Assisi to pray together with him for peace, justice, and the integrity of creation. Christian leaders from the East and West, from the North and the South, from various denominations, Asians like the Dalai Lama, traditional African and American Indian indigenous religious dignitaries with their feathers and amulets—religious believers came together from all over the world.

The Pope did not lead them in their prayers. He asked all of them to pray in their own way, within their own traditions, and from within their own selves. That is what they did. Afterward some people at the Vatican expressed their surprise about what the Holy Father had done. They did not completely agree with his course of action. Some weeks later John Paul II countered their criticism in the Christmas talk of that year, a talk in which he addressed the Cardinals in Rome every year. He told them: "The Holy Spirit is mysteriously present in every human heart."

That same Spirit moved the wise foreigners to follow the star that brought them together from different places. Legend tells us that they came from different parts of the world, from Africa, from Asia, and from Europe. The star brought them together around the child Jesus.

Their coming together to honor the child has been a light for each generation when we celebrate Epiphany. Each of us, and all of us together, are invited to follow the same star.

FOR REFLECTION

- Do you listen carefully to God's voice when following your path through life, as the wise travelers in Matthew's story did? When and how do you do that?

- One of our main challenges nowadays is to be willing to be a good and understanding neighbor to people of other beliefs and convictions. How do you relate to them in everyday life?

- How would you react if invited to pray with others in a non-Christian context?

EVENING PRAYER

Almighty God, help me enliven my realization of the presence of the Spirit you breathed into me and into all of us from the beginning of our lives. Amen.

SECOND DAY

MORNING MEDITATION

"The straight path"

Read Matthew 3:1–17

The people came from all over Judea and the coastal region to John, who had returned from his stay in the desert dressed like an Old Testament prophet, in some animal skins held together with a leather belt. Someone said that he lived on the insects he found in the wilderness. John was standing in the river Jordan, and the line in front of him was very long. He was baptizing the people. They had all come because they, too, like the visitors to the child Jesus in Bethlehem, were full of expectations.

These expectations were deeply rooted in their messianic prophetic hope. John's words echoed those old prophecies when he quoted Isaiah: "A voice cries out: In the wilderness prepare the way of the Lord, make straight in the desert a highway for our God" (40:3). John even added that the kingdom of God was near! He told his listeners to repent, confess their sins, and be baptized; the kingdom of heaven was near. The wilderness of the world in which they lived was going to be transformed. Its crooked ways would be straightened out.

Even Pharisees and Sadducees from Jerusalem joined the crowd, and John addressed them in particular when explaining his mission. He made it clear that the introduction of the new would require the purification of the old. He used strong language to make his point. Every tree that brought forth bad fruits was going to be cut down and burnt. In fact, he said, the axe was already lying as on the root of those trees. Using another image, he warned that all the chaff would be burnt, too. This was the only way to repair the world, and to restore it for the coming reign of God.

In a way John was a bit of a letdown. He rendered only a partial spiritual cleaning and cleansing service. He himself said: "I baptize you with water for repentance but one who is more powerful than I...will baptize you with the Holy Spirit and fire" (3:11). John could only provide the first part, the introductory part of the transformation to come.

This two-part "ritual" might remind us, in a sense, of our own baptismal ceremony. Baptism, too, consists of two actions. The minister of baptism pours the water on the person being baptized, in the name of the Father, the Son, and the Holy Spirit. The second action may sometimes be overlooked in its importance, if only because "baptism" refers being cleansed with life-giving water.

In the second part of baptism the one who baptizes dips his thumb in oil blessed during Holy Week and anoints the one baptized, while he says, "I am anointing you as Jesus was anointed priest, prophet, and king." Later on in life this reality is "confirmed" by the sacrament of confirmation. All of us are baptized in water, the Holy Spirit, and fire!

John continued his ministry and baptized those who came to him. Then one day Jesus was in the line of those waiting to be baptized by John. To express his solidarity with all of us, he waited his turn. Finally he stepped into the water in front of John, the same John who had leaped in the womb of his mother Elizabeth when she met Mary who was pregnant with Jesus years before. When he recognized Jesus, John hesitated and told Jesus: "I need to be baptized by you and do you come to me?" Or in other words, "I am not going to baptize you; you should baptize me."

At that moment we hear Jesus speak his first words in Matthew's gospel. He says: "Let is be so now, for it is proper for us in this way to fulfill all righteousness." Matthew uses the Greek word for that last word "righteousness," namely *dikaiosune*. Our text translates it as righteousness; it could also be translated as "justice." It is a word Matthew uses seven times in his gospel, twice in the beatitudes, and five times in the Sermon on the Mount.

Using the word righteousness, Jesus reminds John of what John himself had said to the crowd that came to be baptized. John had spoken of "the straight path," the path which would lead to the reign of God. This path was to lead to that hoped-for reality, the fulfillment of the messianic prophecies, the restoration and renewal of the world. It would "lead our feet into the way of peace," as John the Baptist's father Zechariah had said at the circumcision of his son (cf Lk 1:79).

In the twenty-eight chapters of Matthew's gospel there are thirty-five references to justice, which is the only straight path toward the reign of God and its peace. Jesus himself would make that very clear when he said later on: "For I tell you, unless your righteousness exceeds that of the scribes and Pharisees, you will never enter the kingdom of heaven" (5:20).

In the end John agreed to baptize Jesus. When Jesus came out of the water, heaven opened and the Spirit of God descended "like a dove alighting on him." A voice from heaven said, "This is my Son, the Beloved, with whom I am well pleased."

The renewal of the world and humanity had begun. The path began to be straightened out.

FOR REFLECTION

- Reflect for some time on the two moments in your own baptism: the cleansing (and life-giving) water and being anointed as Jesus was anointed, priest, prophet, and king.

- Do you walk on the "straight path" of righteousness? How can you help bring about God's reign in your life and in the world?

MORNING PRAYER

Loving God, help me understand who I am,
and what my responsibilities are.
Assist me in the renewal of my world so it will witness to the triumph of
your justice and peace. Amen.

FAITH RESPONSE FOR TODAY

Straighten out a "crooked area" in your path.

EVENING MEDITATION

"Tempted by the devil"

Read Matthew 4:1–11

Matthew's gospel tells us that the Holy Spirit led Jesus into the desert. In the desert a human being is alone and, in a way, isolated. The desert changes all the time, untouched by human hands, virginal and pristine. But, in the mind and imagination of the biblical authors—and not only for them—it also represents a place of evil spirits, demons, and trials.

The Jewish people had been tested for forty years in the desert. Moses had dwelt there alone for forty days before he received the new law, the Ten Commandments. John the Baptizer came from the desert to begin his mission at the river Jordan.

In the desert, Jesus, too, was tempted, challenged, and tested by Satan. Matthew does not tell us much about Satan. What he does say is that the devil desperately wants to obstruct and undo the coming of the reign of God in our world. Satan is presented as the opponent of righteousness and peace, not only in the desert and in the life of Jesus, but also in the wilderness of the world we live in, as individuals and as a community.

In being tempted, and in the way he is tempted, Jesus really became like one of us. As the author of the letter to the Hebrews would later write: "For we do not have a high priest who is unable to sympathize with our weaknesses, but we have one who in every respect has been tested as we are, yet without sin" (4:15). Resisting Satan, his tempter, Jesus remains a model for all of us.

The story begins after Jesus had been fasting in the desert for forty days. He was hungry, and the devil tempts him by suggesting that he might use his power to ease his own hunger. "If you are the Son of God, [if you are the one you say you are, help yourself and] command these stones to become loaves of bread." Use your power, use your influence as the Son of God for your own advantage only, for yourself alone.

It is the type of temptation we often face when we have to make a decision in which we weigh our own interests against the interests of others. It happens during an argument when someone says something like, "Let us be logical," "Let us be rational and reasonable," or "Business is business," knowing perfectly well that by acting this way other people will be betrayed, and a more important value will be lost.

This kind of temptation occurred again in Jesus' life. When he was hanging on the cross, the crowd mocked and tempted him: "If you are the Son of God, come down from the cross—and we will believe!" (27: 40, 42). Of course they would have believed in him if he had done that. He would have been just like those who were shouting at him, accustomed only to think of themselves. He would have been—so to speak—"howling with the wolves" in the wilderness of the world, thinking only of himself and overlooking his messianic mission. He would have been swayed by egoism, greed, and consumerism, like persons catering only for themselves and overlooking everyone else. Giving in to the temptation would have been the only sensible thing to do, according to their way of thinking.

Jesus resisted the devil's first attempt to veer him away from his mission. He told the devil, "One does not live by bread alone"; there is more at stake than just that. One should be faithful to God's word and will.

Hearing Jesus speak about his relationship to God, the devil tried to profit by Jesus' confidence in God when he proposes his second temptation. Taking Jesus to the pinnacle of the temple, Satan asked him to show his trust in God by throwing himself down, for—and the devil quotes from the Bible—would God not send his angels "to bear you up"? Jesus refused, also quoting Scripture: "Do not put the Lord your God to the test."

Your trust in God should be such that testing your confidence in God, testing God's trust would be totally inappropriate. If you really trust someone you would not even think of such a test. Asking for proof would betray your lack of confidence.

Having failed again the devil presented his final temptation. Putting Jesus on a mountaintop, Satan showed him all the kingdoms of the world, telling Jesus that he would give him all that power if Jesus would worship him. This temptation is about using power or force to attain one's goal, the temptation to take over the world in one enormous swoop, and to do so, without consideration of others, without any loss of time, and without any involvement or participation by others.

This temptation, too, returned in Jesus' life, for instance, when one of his disciples (Peter) drew his sword trying to defend Jesus, meanwhile slicing off the ear of one of the high priest's servants. Jesus stopped him, saying: "Put your sword back into its place; for all who take the sword will perish by the sword" (26:51–52). Jesus refused to use violence. The reign of God was going to be brought about another way.

It is not difficult to see how these three temptations or tests occur in our own lives and in the life of our communities. We can determine how they should be tackled if we want to follow Jesus' example.

We should, however, not view such temptations in a merely negative way. Matthew does not describe them as such in Jesus' life. They are real challenges, tests that help us see what we should do and not do— where we risk being trapped and how to escape from those traps.

FOR REFLECTION

- Do you recognize in your own life the same kind of temptations Jesus faced?

- Meditate for some time on these words from the letter of James, on trials: "My brothers and sisters, whenever you face trials of any kind, consider it nothing but joy, because you know that the testing of your faith produces endurance; and let endurance have its full effect, so that you may be mature and complete, lacking in nothing" (1:2–4).

- Having experienced temptation himself, Jesus advised us to pray: "Do not bring us to the time of trial" (9:12), or "not lead us into temptation."

EVENING PRAYER

Almighty God, help me be more like Jesus, who confidently put his life in your hands. Amen.

THIRD DAY

MORNING MEDITATION

"Great crowds followed him"

Read Matthew 4:23–25

Once Jesus had heard that John the Baptist had been arrested, he left Nazareth and settled in Capernaum. There he repeated John the Baptist's message: "Repent, for the kingdom of heaven has come near!" There was a difference however. John had spoken of it as a prophecy; Jesus spoke of it as an actual fact. The kingdom had begun! It started with a trickle, two fishermen, and then another two. In no time a crowd started to surround him. The first persons he invited, the others came without invitation. They came on their own; they did not need an invitation.

Those he chose to be his close cooperators, his apostles, were a very diverse group. They included someone like Matthew, who as a tax-gatherer was a collaborator with the occupying Roman government. But there was also Simon, not the one he nicknamed Peter, but Simon the Canaanite, who was called a Zealot in Luke's gospel (6:15). This name means that he belonged to one of the most nationalist of all nationalist Jewish groups in those days, a kind of freedom fighter.

In his commentary on this diversity William Barclay tells us in his *New Testament Commentary*: "The plain fact is that if Simon the Zealot had met Matthew the tax-gatherer anywhere else than in the company of Jesus, he would have stuck a dagger in him." In their devotion to Jesus the two could sit at the same table, and so could the mystically inclined John together with the sword-carrying (and wielding) Peter. Love for Jesus brought together people who otherwise would have been each other's opposites and even enemies.

Jesus believed in shared responsibility; he did not hesitate to delegate his mission in this world to others. He had overcome the temptation to power in the desert. He intended to involve all of them—and all of us—in the process he initiated in this world. From the beginning he intended it to be a corporate kind of enterprise.

So, the initial trickle of followers became a crowd, and in no time a mass of people surrounded him, a crowd that was growing all the time. Jesus did something to those who surrounded him. They listened to him. They looked at him. They tried to touch him. Something seemed to vibrate in them when they did this. They heard the melody he sang in their own hearts. That was how they recognized Jesus as someone special, and that is why so many followed him wherever he went. It is the reason why they "converted" to him and changed their lives!

Yet not everyone followed Jesus. Some came to trap him. They asked for more signs, as Satan had done standing with him on the temple's pinnacle. Yet, the continually growing crowds came because they felt empowered by him.

Jesus revealed to them that there are immense depths in all of us, fantastic possibilities, realities that remain hidden unless someone else stimulates us. Had John the Baptist not said that Jesus came to baptize us with the Holy Spirit and fire (3:11)? Why were those others asking for more signs? Did they not notice the light that entered the lives of those who let themselves be affected by Jesus? Did they not see how these people changed the direction of their lives? Did they not realize that those who followed Jesus were taken up in the process he launched in our world, its restoration into the reign of God, a reign of justice and peace?

Was it, perhaps, their impatience that made them blind? Had they been expecting that the change would come through an enormous, sudden, and instantaneous intervention from heaven, possibly even a violent one, as many believers in Jesus expect even in our own day?

The Jesus whom Matthew describes answers those questions in many ways. Jesus explains again and again that what he came to set in motion was a process; a movement in which all of us would and should be involved and engaged in. He explained this in many different ways. The kingdom of God, or the reign of God (in which past, present and future will be kept together), is like a treasure hidden in a field that still has to be found (13: 44). It is like a fishing net that has been thrown out by fishermen, but still has to be hauled in (13:47–48). It is like a pearl people want to buy, but they still have to sell a lot before they will be able to pay the price (13:46).

The kingdom of God will be fully realized when we have finished our task. Yet, it is already breaking through again and again as we work at it, pray for it, live it in our daily lives, and celebrate it when we are sitting with him and each other at the Lord's table. As we break his bread and share his wine, the body and blood of our Lord and brother Jesus Christ, we find a foretaste of the great gathering promised at the end of time, when the work has been done (8:11).

Matthew not only leaves us with a description of Jesus going about in his ministry, surrounded by great crowds of people (4:23–25). He also briefs us on the job description Jesus left us.

FOR REFLECTION

- Does praying "your kingdom come" have any direct influence on the way you live your life and make your decisions?

- Are you aware of being taken up in a process that should change the face of the earth in a messianic, that is, redemptive and restorative way?

- Jesus brought people together who were very different from each other economically, socially, culturally, but also politically. What is the significance of his example in our day and age?

MORNING PRAYER

Loving God, help me to be challenged by the life and message of your Son to join him in the transformation of the world. Amen.

FAITH RESPONSE FOR THIS DAY

Compliment someone whose insights you do not always appreciate, for a positive contribution she or he has made to the common good.

EVENING MEDITATION

"Blessed are they"

Read Matthew 5:1–16

Seeing the crowd that surrounds him full of hope and expectation, Jesus climbs a mountain—most probably a high hill—and he begins to teach them. He begins his Sermon on the Mount with the eight Beatitudes. There is a ninth one but it is of another type, and does not fit so very well with the eight others:

"Blessed are the poor in spirit, for theirs is the kingdom of heaven.

Blessed are those who mourn, for they will be comforted.

Blessed are the meek, for they will inherit the earth.

Blessed are those who hunger and thirst for righteousness, for they will be filled.

Blessed are the merciful, for they will receive mercy.

Blessed are the pure in heart, for they will see God.

Blessed are the peacemakers, for they will be called children of God.

Blessed are those who are persecuted for righteousness sake, for there is the kingdom of heaven."

The first and the last of those Beatitudes are in the present tense. The six others refer to the future.

As we noted earlier we also find the first one in Luke's gospel, but while Luke's Jesus says: "Blessed are the poor," Matthew's Jesus says: "Blessed are the poor in spirit." That's quite a difference! As we noted in our introduction to this retreat, Matthew was probably not addressing poor people. There are other indications in his gospel that his readers were relatively well off. They were not poor in the literal sense of the word. We find a good description of the poor in the book of Habakkuk 3:17–18:

"Though the fig tree does not blossom,
  and no fruit is on the vines;
  though the produce of the olive fails,
  and the fields yield no food;
  and there is no herd in the stalls,
  yet I will rejoice in the Lord;
I will exult in the God of my salvation."

Most probably very few of Matthew's readers would have identified with the poor as described here, just like hardly any one of us would either. So what did this "poor in spirit" mean? Who was Jesus thinking of when he spoke of them? Are they persons who are rather well off, or very well off, but who nevertheless are detached, selfless, kind, and compassionate? Perhaps, but there is also another possible answer to the question.

"The poor in spirit" are not called such for economic reasons but because they are aware of their need for God and of the fact that they and the peoples of the world do not yet practice the kind of justice and mercy God calls us all to. The face of the earth still has to be changed! The process is not over. Humanity's messianic expectations have yet to be met. The world as it is, is not the fulfillment of the kingdom.

The poor in spirit are those who know and feel that, notwithstanding all our achievements, successes and advances, the kingdom of God is not yet realized in this world. They sense that, though we might be quite happy about the way we have organized our society, there are too many left out, who suffer, who starve, who are abused. The poor in spirit are the persons who are intent on changing things in view of justice for all. That is why they are so often persecuted, vilified, ridiculed, and sometimes even murdered because of their thirst for righteousness.

The poor in spirit belong to the kingdom of God because they are willing to live in the tension of being in but not of the world. They want to change the world so that the other six beatitudes will be fulfilled, so that this world will be freed of arrogance, homelessness, injustice, darkness, and war.

We have not achieved the reign of God, the restoration of the world as yet. So many prayers still have to be heard, so many paths have still to be straightened, so much of the mission Jesus left to us has still to be accomplished.

The poor in spirit are those who know that we are only on our way! They realize that we have still to go through the crucible of the love Jesus showed us on the cross!

This first Beatitude is in the present tense because people of this mindset—the poor in spirit—are the hope of the world! The eighth Beatitude is also in the present tense: Blessed are those who—at the moment—are suffering persecution because they are actually changing what is necessary to accomplish the mission of justice, peace, and love left to us by Jesus.

In this way the other six Beatitudes fall into place. Only when this work continues will those who mourn be comforted, will the meek inherit the earth, will those thirsting for justice be filled, will those who are merciful receive mercy, will those who are pure of heart see God, and will the peacemakers be called children of God.

In the end Jesus added a ninth Beatitude, saying blessed are you when you are reviled and persecuted on my account, because of my message, for your reward will be great. You will be persecuted like the prophets of old, but do not forget you are the salt of the earth and the hope and light of the world (cf 5:11–14).

FOR REFLECTION

- Do you consider yourself as someone who is "poor in spirit"? Does your vocation as a disciple of Jesus influence your vision of the future of our world?

- What do you think of those Christians who maintain that justice and peace issues are beyond the scope of the Church's spiritual and religious mission?

- Did you ever think of supporting organizations like The Catholic Campaign for Human Development, Pax Christi, Bread for the World, Care, Amnesty International, or any organization like that?

EVENING PRAYER

Almighty God, may my life be worthy of the life you have in store for us.
Amen.

FOURTH DAY

MORNING MEDITATION

"One Father of all"

Read Matthew 5:17 to 7:28

The Sermon on the Mount, which begins with the eight Beatitudes, is filled with advice on how to form a community. It is about issues that in our days are as actual as they must have been at the time of Jesus. It talks about anger, marriage, oath taking, juridical litigation, how to help our brothers and sisters in need, how to deal with enemies who threaten us, how to pray, how to overcome worry, ending with what is called "the golden rule" and a warning against self-deception.

A striking aspect of Matthew's sermon is the frequent use Jesus makes of the name "Father" for God: over thirty times. He speaks about "My Father" (eight times), "Your Father" (eight times), "Their Father" (once) and "our Father" (once). Mark's gospel, instead, only uses the name "Father" for God twice.

Why would Matthew insist so much on the use of that title? Did it have something to do with the specific problems of the group he addressed in his version of the Good News? He wrote for a group of Christians who no longer lived in Jerusalem, as they had done for years. Because of political developments and the fall of Jerusalem, they had had to leave Jerusalem and were now living in diaspora, in exile, as strangers in a foreign environment. How should they relate to the people among whom they dwelled?

This issue had already been discussed at the First Council of Jerusalem (cf Acts 15:1–18). Now strangers, people of various faiths and beliefs, surrounded them.

Christians all over the world are facing this situation more and more. Homogeneous societies are disappearing rapidly. Mosques and temples are built, and at the same time church buildings are closing and disappearing. You do not need to be an expert to foresee the danger of cultural and religious wars. Our daily news is full of interreligious difficulties, terrorism, conflict, and trouble.

An old Bible story tells us how Noah's seventy-two grandsons left their grandfather's homestead years after the flood, spreading all over the earth. They walked away from each other, each family having its own history and developing its own culture. They walked further and further away from each other on a globe where they were bound to meet again one day. We are living that day. You can see it in cities all over the world.

During the Second Vatican Council, about forty years ago already, for the first time the whole world was represented. Two of the documents of that Council referred explicitly to this new situation in the world and in the church. The first of those documents appropriately began "In this age of ours...". This *Declaration on the Relation of the Church to Non-Christian Religions* spoke about the need of healthy interreligious collaboration and dialogue. The second one, titled *Declaration on Religious Liberty* insisted on the need for interreligious respect and freedom.

In this context Matthew's insistence on God as our common source of existence acquires a new relevance and significance. Jesus asked us in his Sermon on the Mount to pray, saying, "Our Father" (6:9), in a context where the word "our" does not refer only to our own circle or group, but to the whole of humankind.

We have to love our enemies because they are children of the same Father (5:45). We should greet them as our brothers and sisters because of the common origin we have in the same life-giver. We should be perfect as our common Father is perfect (5:48) loving everyone, providing all of us with the rain and sun (5:45) we all equally need. It is into all of us that God breathed "the breath of life" (Gen 2:7). This divine breath continues to support our lives.

At the moment humanity, divided against itself, is scattered all over the world. Jesus came to bring us together again, restoring our relationships, healing where healing is necessary, giving us the power to forgive if forgiveness is needed. Jesus came "to gather" us together into one (12:30, 23:37), restoring the old, broken common bond.

In Matthew's gospel Jesus calls the ones who are already gathered together in him, "his household" (10:25) and his "church" (16:18, 18:17), calling himself "the master of the house," or in other translations the "householder." In one of his parables he compares himself to a son sent to take charge of his Father's business (21:33–41).

Did he not promise to live up to his name Emmanuel, "God with us" and to accompany us always, until the end of time (28:20)?

FOR REFLECTION

• The word "church" relates to the Greek word for "house." Did you ever reflect on the fact that Jesus calls the church his household and himself the master of the house? What implications would you draw from the words he uses?

• Read Matthew 18:15–20 on fraternal correction in Jesus' household and on praying together with two or three brothers and sisters.

• Simone Weil, the French mystic who wrote about prayer, referred to this saying of Jesus about the "two or three" and added, "Two or three, there should be no more." She did not intend to exclude praying with a larger group, but she wanted to stress what Jesus said himself, that when two or three come together to pray, their prayer has a special power. Anyone who has ever prayed like that at a sick bed, at a happy or sad occasion, experiences this. A father and a mother, a sister and a brother, a friend with a friend—every time two or three pray together—they will notice Jesus' presence. We often overlook this type of prayer. It shows us how good the Lord is and how he is present among us.

MORNING PRAYER

Our Father in heaven, hallowed be your name. Your kingdom come. Your will be done on earth as it is in heaven. Help us to prepare ourselves that we might gather together your human family. Amen.

FAITH RESPONSE FOR TODAY

Apply today one of the suggestions made by the 1991 Vatican document on dialogue. It suggests among other things that in our interreligious contacts we try, 1. the dialogue of life, by simply being good neighbors; 2. the dialogue of action, trying to solve our societal problems together with others; 3. the dialogue of religious experience, for instance, by an exchange about our life of prayer.

EVENING MEDITATION

"The Father's Spirit speaking through you"
Read Matthew 7:24–29

While listening to Jesus during his Sermon on the Mount, "the crowds were astounded at his teaching, for he taught them as one having authority, and not as their scribes" (7:29). They realized that what he said did not come from a source outside of himself, as it did for their scribes who based themselves on the law, but on something that came from within himself. He was moved from within. The same crowds would express this very impression in an even stronger way on another occasion when "they glorified God, who had given such authority to human beings" (9:8). Listening to him and witnessing him moved them, too, from within! His approach made them grow!

The scribes had also been listening. They, too, were amazed and even upset about what was going on. They approached Jesus to challenge his authority. They came to him with their doubts, asking him: "By what authority are you doing these things, and who gave you this authority?" (21:23–27).

Jesus answered them, as he almost always did, by asking them a question in turn. He asked them where they thought the baptism of John the Baptizer came from; did it have a divine or a human origin? They refused to answer him. They did not want to admit that it had a divine origin because Jesus would have asked them: "Then why did you not believe him?" They did not want to admit either that they thought John's authority had been human because they did not want a conflict with the crowd, who regarded John as a prophet.

Since they refused to answer him, Jesus did not answer their question either. However, it is rather obvious what his answer would have been. His authority came from God, the Spirit of God within himself, as the crowds knew when they glorified God for having given him such authority, healing, telling his story in a way that deeply moved them, repairing and reconciling human and divine relationships, forgiving and teaching. The crowds knew, they intuited, that Jesus was "online" with God, guided by God's Spirit from within and not just by a law from without (cf Gal 5:18). Yet, to avoid all misunderstandings, Jesus had explained his relation to the established, God-given Law. With his new teaching, how did he relate to the old Jewish law and tradition? In fact, Jesus begins giving that explanation from the very moment of his public appearance in Matthew's gospel. The very first words Jesus speaks in Matthew's gospel are, "Let it be so now; for it is proper for us in this way to fulfill all righteousness" (3:15).

Matthew, a Judeo-Christian addressing his fellow Judeo-Christians, stresses again and again that Jesus came to fulfill their own Jewish tradition and law. He mentions four times very explicitly that Jesus came to fulfill what God had said through the prophets (1:22; 8:17; 12:17; 13:35) and that he was the Messiah they had been expecting for so long, (1:16–17; 2:4–6; 11:2–5; 16:16; 25:10; 26:63–64). In fact, Jesus says it even once of himself when "he sternly ordered the disciples not to tell anyone that he was the Messiah" (16:20).

Trying to counteract a possible misunderstanding of his relation to the old law, the prophets, and tradition Jesus openly stated: "Do not think that I have come to abolish the law or the prophets; I have come not to abolish, but to fulfill. For truly I tell you, until heaven and earth pass away, not one letter, not one stroke of a letter, will pass from the law until all is accomplished" (5:17–18). He did, however, introduce a change. Jesus' authority did not derive from the old law, not even from the Mosaic one, though what he stated and what the old regime held coincided on many points. He himself stressed that change every time he contrasted the "you have heard that it was said in ancient times" with the "but I say to you."

What he said went beyond that law, and it came from within himself. It was based on his direct relationship with God. Even when speaking about his listeners and his disciples in Matthew's gospel, Jesus speaks about "the Spirit of your Father speaking through you" (10:20).

The enthusiasm of the crowd that followed Jesus was due to the fact that they met in him someone who treated them in a manner different from their high priests and scribes. Jesus took them seriously. He gave them a hope those authorities did not give them, and did not even want to give them. Jesus did not talk down to them as so many others were accustomed to doing. He treated them as friends and equals. He considered them to be filled with the Spirit of his Father.

In fact, they had to be more realistic about themselves than they had ever been before. They were relating to God in a way they had never experienced before, not only through mediators, but also directly. It would not make their lives easier, but it definitely made their lives more worthwhile. Living in accordance with that Spirit from God within, and recognizing that same Spirit in their communities, would not only be a blessing for them, but also for others.

Just as the crowds around Jesus glorified God because of what they experienced in him, they in their turn would shine as a light before others, who in seeing their good deeds would "glorify their heavenly Father" (5:16), and change their own lives.

FOR REFLECTION

- Meditate for some time on Jesus' saying: "I tell you, unless your righteousness exceeds that of the scribes and Pharisees, you will never enter the kingdom of heaven" (5:20). What does your "conscience" say about the above? Do you allow "the Spirit of the Father [to] speak through you"? (10:20).

- Do you recall moments when someone's deeds made you glorify God? What was the reason? Do you remember whether anyone ever glorified God because of your good deeds?

- Do you ever consult the presence of the Spirit within you when you have to make an important decision? Do you involve others in that kind of discernment of the Spirit?

EVENING PRAYER

Lord Jesus, may we use the gift of the Spirit in such a way that when people see the good we do, they give glory to God. Amen.

FIFTH DAY

MORNING MEDITATION

"Being healed by him"

Read Matthew 8:1–17

Most of the miracles Jesus worked in Matthew's gospel remain untold. There were so many that Matthew could not recount them all. He would just report that they brought the physically and mentally sick to Jesus from every place, and that "he healed all who were sick" (8:16). And Matthew added: "This was to fulfill what had been spoken through the prophet Isaiah: 'He took our infirmities and bore our diseases'" (8:17).

Matthew tells about nine of Jesus' healing miracles in detail. It is interesting to see how in all those stories a mutual relationship develops between the healer and the healed person. Jesus touches those he heals, though not always physically; but they also move him. Every healing is the start of a special relationship. Jesus always involves the healed, or asks them to become involved in one way or other, in his mission here on earth.

Let us consider the three first healings Matthew mentions. The first one is a leper. He told Jesus, "Lord, if you choose, you can make me clean." Jesus stretches out his hand, touches him, and repeating the words the man himself had used, he says: "I do choose. Be made clean!" Immediately something happened to the man's skin; he was healed. But then Jesus adds, "See that you say nothing to anyone; but go, show yourself to the priest and offer the gift that Moses commanded, as a testimony to them" (8:1–4).

The cured man was not even allowed to tell the priest that he had been miraculously healed by Jesus. He only had to show his healed, unblemished skin. In other words, he had to take into account that telling his story might have compromised and hindered Jesus' mission. He was asked to take precautions in his own life to prevent that and to keep his mouth shut. He obviously did not do that; he must have told the story, otherwise we would not even have known about it. But he had been asked to take Jesus' mission into account.

The second miracle is one that was of great importance and interest for the Judeo-Christians who, as refugees from Jerusalem, were surrounded by a people foreign to them. Jesus not only healed the servant of a Roman soldier, he even stated to the Jewish crowd that surrounded him that day, that he was amazed at the soldier's faith. "Truly I tell you in no one in Israel have I found such faith" (8:10). You might consider Jesus' relationship as the beginning of his mission of gathering all nations into the reign of God (8:10–11).

Jesus' third miracle is perhaps the best example of this kind of relationship. It took place when he went home to Capernaum to the house of Simon Peter. Simon Peter's mother-in-law (so Peter must have been married!) was sick in bed with a fever. When Jesus was told that she was sick, he went to her, touched her hand, and the fever left her. The text continues: "and [she] began to serve him" (8:14–15).

Some commentators and preachers have suggested that this meant she just started to prepare a meal for Jesus and served him. Other more serious and informed scholars see this story of the healing of Peter's mother-in-law as a paradigm, a prototype of discipleship. First sick, then saved, she served Jesus and joined him in his mission. Jesus' healing connected the persons he cured to his mission.

Being healed by him involved this risk. That might have been the reason that Jesus sometimes asked the people who came to him to be healed, whether it was really their intention to be healed. Were they willing to accept the consequences?

A question we could ask ourselves during this retreat: Do we really want to be healed, not only from our physical blindness or deafness but from our spiritual and moral shortcomings as well? Do you really want to see? Do you really want to hear? Do you know what you are in for when you start to see? Do you know what you are in for when you start to hear?

We often close ourselves off from our own hopes, griefs, and anxieties and those of others. We act sometimes like children when facing a problem—for example, an injection by a nurse or something like that. We close our eyes as if to say: "If I don't see it, it is not there."

How often we hear people make remarks like, "I don't read the newspaper anymore, I can't stand all the bad news in it." How often do we ourselves may turn the television off so as not to be confronted with the misery, the hunger, the sickness, and the poverty in so many parts of the world and even in our own society?

It is the blindness and the deafness of persons who are unwilling to face the human condition as it is—alcoholics who do not want to recognize that they are addicted; tourists who do not want to notice the poverty of the country they visit; patients who do not accept their sickness; television viewers who never watch a documentary about persons who are neglected in their own country or in the world.

Pope John Paul II repeated a phrase from one of the documents of the Second Vatican Council:

> The joys and hopes, the griefs and anxieties of the people of this age, especially those who are poor or in any way afflicted, these are the joys and the hopes, the griefs and anxieties of the followers of Christ. Indeed, nothing genuinely human fails to raise an echo in their hearts (*Pastoral Constitution on the Church in the Modern World* #1).

If you share in the mission of Jesus, then you are touched by any evil done to a human being, but you are also touched by any good done to a person.

You can't be Jesus' follower and remain blind and deaf to the needs of others, to the situations of injustice, poverty, and oppression in our world. You will have to see with his eyes and hear with his ears. You have to be healed. Jesus asks you, too: "What do you want me to do for you?" Do you want to be healed?

FOR REFLECTION

• How would you answer Jesus' question, "What do you want me to do for you?" (Mk 10:51)

- A popular hymn uses the words of one of the psalms: "The Lord hears the cry of the poor." Do those words have an impact on your life?

- Did you ever have a healing influence on someone?

MORNING PRAYER

Dear Jesus, may my life be in line with Jesus' love for his brothers and sisters. Help me share his healing compassion. Amen.

FAITH RESPONSE FOR TODAY

Arrange to visit a sick family member, neighbor, or colleague.

EVENING MEDITATION

"Should you not have had mercy?"

Read Matthew 18:21–35

The road that leads to the fulfillment of the reign of God among us is a difficult one, and the journey is full of challenges. We will fall and rise again. The journey will involve both betrayal and faithfulness. We will reach the end, but the way will sometimes be messy. Jesus explained this and warned us about it when he told the parable of the wheat and the weeds. He compared the kingdom of God to a farmer who sowed good seed on his land. But in the dark of the night, while everyone was asleep, an enemy sowed weeds to destroy the farmer's crop.

The wheat and weeds grew together. When the servants asked the owner if they should tear out all the weeds so that the wheat could flourish, the owner of the field refused to give permission. He said, "Let both of them grow until the harvest." He was convinced that the wheat would survive, notwithstanding the enemy's effort to sabotage his plans. It is rather obvious in Matthew's gospel that the enemy is Satan.

As part of the "wheat field" of this world, the Church, too, has a mixture of wheat and weeds. This is the reality as long as we are "on the way," as long as we are "in process."

The apostle Peter is an example of this "process." He protested several times about the road Jesus was going to walk, and in the end he even denied Jesus three times. He was like the mixture of good and bad, of wheat and weeds, that Jesus spoke about.

Perhaps for that very reason Jesus gave him the name Peter, the rock on which the church, the household of Jesus, would be built. Peter represented the substance and reality of the Church. The good prevailed in him, just as it would in the church built on him. The betrayal had been and will be forgiven.

When Simon Peter asked Jesus how often a member of the community should be forgiven for his or her sins, he might also have been thinking of himself. How often would he himself be forgiven? Up to seven times? Jesus answered him, "Not seven times, but, I tell you, seventy times seven times" (18:22). Or to phrase it more colloquially, Jesus answered him, "You must be joking; seven times would not do. You would not make it. Nobody would." There is no limit to forgiveness. And there is no point at which we can say, "We have forgiven enough."

In Matthew's version of Jesus' parable about the lost sheep, the shepherd does not lose the sheep; the sheep goes astray. The sheep leaves the shepherd. The sheep causes the problem, yet the shepherd leaves all the others on the mountaintop to look for the stray one. Jesus adds, "So it is not the will of your Father in heaven that one of these little ones should be lost" (18:10–14).

Jesus asks us to share in our Father's mercy and love, to be merciful as God is merciful, to find the stray sheep, the stray member in our community. First we do it on our own, then with two or three other persons. If that does not help, we involve the whole community. Jesus delegates this task to each of his followers. He does not leave it to the church leadership, but to the whole community. Each and every one of us are to share in God's mercy. We are invited to be merciful as the Father is merciful. Every follower of Jesus Christ is asked to fulfill the office of the good shepherd!

We should be faithful to showing this mercy and forgiveness even if such mercy does not bring the stray back into the community. Jesus told us what to do in that case: "If the offender refuses to listen even to the church, let such a one be to you as a Gentile and a tax collector" (18:17). This does not mean that the persons are totally lost. All of them remain sheltered under God's love, who does not will that any of "these little ones" goes astray and is lost.

Jesus illustrated what he wanted to say and confirmed it in another parable. He compared the kingdom of God to a king who had a servant who owed him an enormous amount of money, ten thousand talents. A talent was worth more than fifteen years' wages of a laborer, so the amount owed must have been the equivalent of billions of dollars. The king threatened to sell the servant and his family as slaves. However, notwithstanding this enormous, almost unimaginable debt, the king cancelled it when the servant appealed to him. So great is God's mercy!

But then this same servant, whose enormous debt had just been cancelled, had a fellow servant thrown in prison because he could not pay him the pitiful sum of a hundred denarii (a denarii being the usual wage for a day's work).

The king heard about this and called in the servant whose enormous debt he had cancelled. He told the servant, "Should you not have had mercy on your fellow-slave, as I had mercy on you?" The king then had the servant put in prison until he paid his entire debt.

The lesson each of us is asked to draw from this story is clear. We are all indebted to God and in need of his mercy; therefore, we should be merciful as God is and forgive our brothers and sisters. We might need to correct each other, bringing the "stray person" back to the straight path. However, any form of mercilessness, revenge, and vindictiveness is out of the question.

FOR REFLECTION

- Reflect for some time on this part of Matthew's version of the Lord's Prayer: "And forgive us our debts, as we also have forgiven our debtors."

- What does reflection on the following saying of Jesus in Matthew's gospel ask you to do: "If you do not forgive others, neither will your Father forgive your trespasses" (6:14–15)?

- Did you ever refuse forgiveness?

EVENING PRAYER

Loving Father, who has forgiven me so often when I strayed from your ways, help me be merciful to all those whom I meet on my path to you.
Amen.

SIXTH DAY

"How many loaves have you?"

Read Matthew 14:13—15:38

Using an unusual superlative some Scripture commentators have called the four gospels the "eatingest" books in world literature. Not only is it amazing how often Jesus is described as eating and drinking with others, but also that he ate and drank with all kinds of people, with sinners as well as saints. Even his contemporaries remarked on this habit. They called Jesus "a glutton and drunkard" (11:19) and accused him of sitting at table with tax collectors and sinners (9:11).

Jesus himself paid great attention to the importance of meals. He compared the Kingdom of God to a banquet, a feast. At the last supper with his disciples he told them: "I will never again drink of this fruit of the vine until that day when I drink it new with you in my Father's kingdom" (26:29).

He would agree with one of the great American authors on eating and drinking, Mary Frances Kennedy, the author of *The Art of Eating,* who wrote in the introduction: "The Gastronomical Me."

"There is a communion of more than bodies when bread is broken and wine is drunk. And that is my answer when people ask me why do you write about hunger, and not wars and love."

Jesus had a dream. It was God the Father's dream—just as it is the dream of every human father and mother for their own family—to see the whole of the human family together at one table, sharing their lives together, and at the same time uniting themselves with the rest of creation, eating and drinking the substance of life and creation itself.

Jesus took on this very human reality at his incarnation. He loved to be at table with others. He even loved to eat with others when those tables were not available. One of the miracles described by all four evangelists is that of the enormous picnics Jesus had with the crowds out on the open hillsides or fields, providing bread and fish for all of them. In one case the men present numbered 5,000, and in the second case 4,000, besides the even greater numbers of women and children.

Facing the hungry crowds Jesus felt compassion for them. His disciples were wondering how to feed the crowd before they would turn home, and Jesus told them "to give them something to eat" (14:17). In both cases they were immediately willing to share what they had, either five loaves of bread and two fish or seven loaves and a few fish. On both occasions Jesus asked the crowds to sit down—some crowd control seemed to be needed. He gave thanks, blessed the food and gave it back to his disciples. "And the disciples gave [the food] to the crowds" (14:19, 15:36).

At the first feeding of the crowd, the "doggy bags" left over were twelve full baskets, and at the second one there were seven baskets of leftovers. Some commentators attach to those numbers a symbolic meaning. The twelve indicated that the twelve tribes of Israel would be eating together in the future kingdom of God; the seven stood for "everyone," "all together."

These two miracles in Matthew were the only ones in which Jesus directly involved the disciples. In most of the other miracles in Matthew's gospel the disciples are not even mentioned. Jesus performed the miracles on his own. When the disciples are mentioned, they play no part in the miracle. Instead, at the miracle of the loaves and fishes, they do take part! Without any objection they provide the food they actually have with them. After having blessed the food, Jesus has the disciples distribute it to the crowds. In this way they are an example for all of us!

FOR REFLECTION

- How would you relate the miracles of "the feeding of the multitudes" in the gospel of Matthew to the following quote from the Second Vatican Council?

  "Wherever there are people in need of food and drink, clothing, housing, medicine, employment, education; wherever people lack the facilities necessary for living a truly human life or are afflicted with serious distress or suffer exile or imprisonment, there Christian charity should seek them out and find them, console them with great solicitude and help them with appropriate relief." (*Decree on the Apostolate of the Laity* #8)

- Do you agree that eating is an activity that unites you with the whole of humanity? If so, what are the spiritual consequences of this insight?

- Should we as "eaters" and "consumers" consider ourselves responsible for the care of the earth and its resources?

MORNING PRAYER

Jesus, who dreamed of gathering us together at the table of your Father, bless the efforts of all those who are engaged in that work. Amen.

FAITH RESPONSE FOR TODAY

Send a donation to an organization that provides food
for the hungry of the world.

EVENING MEDITATION

"He was transfigured before them"
Read Matthew 17:1–13

It was their peak religious experience, in more ways than one. Jesus had taken Peter, James, and John with him up a high mountain by themselves. There he was transfigured in front of them. The three disciples saw Jesus shine like the sun, his face beaming with light. They saw him in his future, risen state. Looking at him, they were at the same time looking at themselves in their own future condition. Jesus showed them who he really was. He also showed them who we are going to become. He showed them our future glory and destiny, the glory and destiny meant for every human being. In his light they started to be light themselves.

Jesus did not remain alone. Moses appeared, the one who had led his people out of their exile, and Elijah the prophet. The three talked to one another; they were discussing something. It is only afterwards, when Jesus and the disciples climbed down the mountain, that we are told what the conversation was about: Jesus' suffering, death, and resurrection; how "the Son of Man is about to suffer" (17:12), and how he would be "raised from the dead" (17:9).

While on that mountaintop Peter was so taken up by what he was experiencing that he forgot about anything and anyone else. He said to Jesus, "Lord, it is good for us to be here; if you wish, I will make three dwellings here" (17:4). He thought, "This is it!" Let us keep it like this.

There was no reaction to his suggestion. He was interrupted by a voice that came from a cloud—often a sign of God's presence in Scripture—repeating what God had said at Jesus' baptism, "This is my Son, the Beloved; with him I am well pleased." The voice added, "Listen to him!" (17:5).

This was all too much for the three disciples. They fell to the ground, overcome by fear, until Jesus touched them saying, "Get up and do not be afraid." When Jesus did that, they looked up and saw that he was alone. Together they climbed down the mountain, back to their everyday life, on their way with him to Jerusalem.

There are many lessons to draw from this story. Jesus had brought the three disciples up the mountain not only to see him in his resurrected glory, but also to be in the company of Moses and Elijah, for all practical purposes to be "in heaven" together with them, and even hear the voice of God. It had been too much for them; for they fell to the ground. The experience left them speechless.

The hand of Jesus raised them up so they could return with him to their ordinary life. This Jesus was no longer the Jesus "of glory"; he was by himself again, alone.

This was the kind of experience that all those who were ever touched by God mystically have gone through. Teresa of Avila, for example, in her book *The Interior Castle* describes how to get in direct touch with God within you. She explains how the road to God's presence is long and sometimes difficult. However, she also makes it clear that those who have made that contact are always almost immediately sent back into their ordinary daily life, to their ordinary tasks on their way to the final end of their journey, biblically described as the heavenly Jerusalem, the reign of God.

Our path to Easter glory, foreshadowed in those peak experiences, will lead us back from the mountaintop down to the plain—and to our everyday life with its work, difficulties, joys, and sufferings.

Religious experience and daily tasks always have to remain inseparable. They belong together. Without having now and then a clear vision of our final destiny, our everyday existence would be depressing and, in a way, desperate. On the other hand, having the vision without walking the walk of our daily life would be an empty experience as well.

Too often it happens that the two remain separated in human life. Too many people go through their days without any further vision and hope. As the prophets of old have said, "Without vision people perish" (cf, e.g., Hosea 4:6). But those who are only interested in the extraordinary, in apparitions and visions, and who overlook the relevance of their presence in the world are not much better off.

Something else happened on that mountaintop that is of special relevance in our day and age. It happened that not only Jesus started to shine, not only his face was lit by glory. His clothes became dazzling white! What does this tell us? The whole creation will be raised up in glory.

In the discussion that Peter, James, and John have with Jesus, Jesus remarks that all things will be restored (17:11). There is an ecological conclusion to be drawn here. We have to be respectful, too, of the rest of nature.

We have many reasons to continue to discuss what our final destiny and rising from the dead could mean for us. We should also consider what it means for the environment we are so closely connected with and even composed of. The resurrection of the body and our final glory might imply much more than we ever thought.

FOR REFLECTION

- Do your religious and faith experiences transform your daily tasks?

- How does Jesus' saying: "Not everyone who says to me, 'Lord, Lord,' will enter the kingdom of heaven, but only who does the will of my Father in heaven" (7:21) relate to the transfiguration story?

- Meditate for some moments on this saying of George Eliot: "Justice is like the Kingdom of God. It is not without us as a fact, it is within us as a great yearning!"

EVENING PRAYER

Loving Father, who forgave me so often when I strayed from your ways, help me be merciful to all those whom I meet on my path to you. Amen.

SEVENTH DAY

MORNING MEDITATION

"This is my body"

Read Matthew 26:1–46

When Jesus had his last supper with the disciples before his arrest, he knew what was going to happen to him. He had told them a few days before: "You know that after two days the Passover is coming, and the Son of Man will be handed over to be crucified" (26:1). When a woman came to anoint him that day, and his disciples thought it a waste of money, he warned them: "By pouring this anointment on my body, she has prepared me for burial" (26:12).

Jesus was no victim of circumstances beyond his control. He could have easily escaped the threat. He even knew who his traitor was, sitting with him at that last supper. What was going to happen was not only something he foresaw; it was something he willed. What he wanted was "to deliver" himself to the effects and the outcome of human sin in the world which he came to redeem and restore. He wanted the effect of human sin on the world to do what it could, which, in the final instance, is to murder and to kill. He was engaging himself in a struggle that had begun even before his struggle with Satan in the desert.

An angel had already informed his foster father Joseph in his dream about Jesus' intentions. It is a story only Matthew tells. Only in Matthew's gospel is the name for the child to be born from Mary, Jesus, fully explained: "You are to name him Jesus, for he will save his people from their sins" (1:21).

In a way the battle had already begun when Herod had tried to do away with the child Jesus by murdering all the babies in Bethlehem. It was the struggle he had had when the devil tested him in the desert. The words Satan used there in the wilderness are heard here again, as the passersby shout at him dying on the cross: "If you are the Son of God, come down from the cross" (27:40). "He saved others; he cannot save himself.... Let him come down from the cross now, and we will believe in him" (27:42).

In his story Matthew emphasizes that the main persons in this drama began to understand what was happening. He is the only one who reports Judas' cry: "I have sinned by betraying innocent blood" (27:4). He is also the only who mentions how Pilate's wife sends Pilate a warning: "Have nothing to do with that innocent man, for today I have suffered a great deal because of a dream about him" (27:19). And in his narrative even Pilate himself wants to dissociate himself from the whole matter: "He took some water and washed his hands before the crowd saying: 'I am innocent of this man's blood, see to it yourselves'" (27:24).

It was only noontime but heaven darkened; it was three in the afternoon when Jesus shouted: "My God, my God why have you forsaken me?" These words express his real anguish and, at the same time, his trust in his Father, who would rescue him in a way none of the bystanders expected.

The signs that followed gave God's answer to Jesus' cry. The earth shook and rocks were split. Tombs opened and many dead persons rose from them. The curtain in the temple was torn from top to bottom. God's final answer to Jesus' last cry was given when Jesus appeared some days later. He had risen from the dead.

The victory had been won over all evil. That evil was not only original sin, or our personal and communal sinfulness. When Jesus was tempted in the desert, an outside power was tempting him, just as it had tempted the first human couple in paradise. Not all the evil in the world can be laid at the door of that first sin of Adam and Eve in the garden.

The most ancient view of the cross is that Christ won a victory over all the powers of evil. They did their worst but could not destroy him because he rose again. Evil, sin, and its consequences were overcome. A new era had started. A new humanity broke through. It was a newness that would affect the whole of that humanity.

It did so immediately. The Roman officer in charge of the crucifixion said: "Truly this man was God's Son" (27:54). There could have been no better expression for recognizing the newness Jesus had brought to the world. Jesus' death on the cross had begun the great gathering together of all the nations of the earth!

When Jesus broke the bread and shared his wine on the night of his last supper before his arrest and death on the cross, he said to his disciples: "Take, eat, this is my body…drink from it, all of you, for this is my blood!" At that moment he united himself with them, just as he does with us when we celebrate the Eucharist. Saint Augustine once wrote, in a text quoted in the *Catechism of the Catholic Church*: "If you want to know what the body of Christ is, hear what the Apostle tells believers: 'You are Christ's body and his members' (1 Cor 12:27)" (#1396).

Jesus' cross, resurrection, and mission are nearer to our hearts than we often think about and live. It is in our lives that we have to manifest and proclaim his cross, resurrection, and mission "until he comes" (1 Cor 11:26).

FOR REFLECTION

- How does your meditation on the cross influence the way you live?

- Do you know anyone who truly follows or has followed Christ's example of giving his or her life for others?

- Why do you think so many people wear a little cross on a chain? What are they trying to tell themselves?

MORNING PRAYER

Loving God, help us do what is just, as responsible members of the body of your Son, our Lord and Brother Jesus Christ, even if it means following his example on the cross. Amen.

FAITH RESPONSE FOR TODAY

Participate in the celebration of the Eucharist, receive the Body of Christ, and reflect on the meditation of this morning.

EVENING MEDITATION

"To the end of the age"

Read Matthew 25:31–46 and 28:16–20

Once, Jesus' disciples had a problem they wanted to discuss with him "privately," a question they did not want to discuss with him in the open. It was the question about the end and about his final return. They asked him, "Tell us, when will this be, and what will be the sign of your coming and of the end of the age?" (24:3). This was the same question Matthew's readers asked who had expected him to come at the fall of Jerusalem. They did not get a direct answer. Jesus said: "About that day and hour no one knows…but only the Father." And he began a long discourse that ended with the description of the end, of the last judgment.

In that discourse he returned to their question, "When will we see you?" but he did not speak about the future when he answered it. He turned their question to the past. He turned their question, "When will we see you?" into the query, "When did you see me?" He even repeated that question six, even twelve times.

We do not know when Jesus will finally return in the end, but we do know where we can look in the interval between now and the end. They are the moments when we are merciful, the moments when we are good to others, to our sisters and brothers.

Every time we meet a person in need, a hungry person, a thirsty one, a stranger, a naked one, a sick or imprisoned one, and help them, we meet Jesus. "I was hungry and you gave me food to eat," "I was a refugee and you welcomed me." Only one of the so-called "Seven Works of Mercy" is not mentioned: "Burying the dead." Any time we do one of these acts of mercy, Jesus returns in our lives, as he identifies himself with those prisoners, refugees, sick, hungry, thirsty, naked ones, "the least of our brothers and sisters." Whenever these things happen, "the reign of God" is reestablished, and the door of heaven opens for a moment.

This might seem somewhat unreal or even abstract, a mere figment of the imagination. It is not. It is real even though it might be about simple things: a smile, a greeting, a cup of coffee, a helping hand, education given to children, or a professionally well-rendered service performed without overcharging for it.

Sometimes, however, serving others might involve activities that ask for sheer heroism. This was the case, for example, for the women and men who sheltered Jews during the Second World War at the risk of their own lives. It is the case for so many others in our days who face the same kind of unjust situations all over the world. In this world Jesus can be found in the hungry, the thirsty, the naked, the sick, the unwelcome, and the persons unjustly locked up in prison,

Our mercy will be needed as long as we live in a world tainted by injustice and sin. That is why our works of mercy and our work for justice have to be balanced. Our works of mercy should not hinder our work for justice; and our work for justice should not hinder our works of mercy.

"Righteousness"—one of the first words Jesus used in Matthew's gospel—should not obstruct the "mercy" Jesus spoke of when talking about the last judgment. We should not do the one and neglect the other.

When we meet Jesus for the last time in Matthew's gospel, we meet him together with his disciples. The women, Mary Magdalene and the other Mary, had seen Jesus alive at his empty tomb. Jesus had given them a message for the absent eleven, a final appointment. They were to meet him in Galilee at the mountaintop, a place where they had met before.

When they saw him they worshiped him, though some of them still had their doubts. Jesus approached them and said: "All authority in heaven and on earth has been given to me. Go therefore and make disciples of all nations, baptizing them in the name of the Father, of the Son and of the Holy Spirit, and teaching them to obey everything that I have commanded you. And remember I am with you always, to the end of the age (28:18-30).

This was not the first time that Jesus told the disciples that they shared in his authority (10:1), but he had never made it as clear to them than in these last words. He now spoke about "all authority in heaven and on earth." He told them that by sharing his authority they should continue his messianic mission in the world. He had overcome evil and sin. This Good News had to be told and the consequences of this victory enjoyed by all.

What he said was not a mere command. Going out on that mission was also the result of them sharing in his Spirit!

In its *Decree on the Mission Activity of the Church*, the Second Vatican Council suggested twice that even if Jesus had not given this command, his disciples, that is to say we ourselves, would have felt the urge to carry out this mission because of the life we share with him.

At the last meeting of Jesus with his followers, he assured them that he would be with them (and consequently with us) on this mission of restoring, renewing and redeeming the world until the end, through the action of the Holy Spirit, and to the glory of the Father.

Alleluia! Praise the Lord! Amen.

FOR REFLECTION

• What is the most important insight you have gained during this retreat?

• How do you relate your life, your family life, and your professional activity to the messianic mission Jesus left us?

• Meditate once more on this saying of George Eliot: "Justice is like the Kingdom of God. It is not without us as a fact, it is within us as a great yearning!"

EVENING PRAYER

Dear Jesus, may this retreat with Matthew open me to a deeper understanding of yourself and of my role in life. Amen.

CONCLUSION

His master said to him, "Well done, my good and faithful servant. Since you were faithful in small matters, I will give you great responsibilities. Come, share your master's joy" (Mt 25:23).

Matthew's gospel was addressed to the Judeo-Christians living in the diaspora. They no longer lived in Jerusalem. They were spread out over the Middle East in non-Christian and non-Jewish countries. They had to learn that the blessings given to them were blessings intended for all. The circle had to be opened, to welcome all. Matthew's gospel illustrates this development.

Halfway through this gospel Jesus' disciples hear him say, "Go nowhere among the gentiles, but go rather to the sheep of the house of Israel" (10:5–6). But at the end of his gospel they are sent out to all nations. It is in this new community that God will dwell to the end of the age.

The situation of Matthew's original readership resembles our own situation as followers of Jesus Christ. Even in the oldest centers of Christianity we are living in a world where we are surrounded by people for whom the Good News Jesus brought is really news. They often have never heard about it, or if they have, it has not been sufficient to take away the darkness that so often overshadows the meaningfulness of life. They might know what evil and injustice are; they might even know what is good and righteous; but they have often given up hope that the good will ever overcome the bad. That certainty is given to us by our faith in Jesus Christ, the Son of God, who delivered himself to the power of sin, evil, and death, who did their worst to him; yet he rose again.

Notwithstanding his final victory, he left us with a mission, the task of making his victory over evil known. He wants us to cooperate, participate in the restoration of God's reign. He does not treat us as children for whom everything is already done. He has given us his Spirit, so that once our mission is fulfilled we will be able to say together with him: "We did it! Alleluia, praise the Lord!"

Our work sometimes seems discouraging. Why didn't he accomplish his mission once and for all? It is a question many of us often ask. Why did he not come back? It was the question still the Christians for whom Matthew wrote his gospel.

There is one story in the Old Testament that might help us understand our situation. Matthew did not use it, but it might help us understand his message. The story is about Jonathan who, according to many Scripture scholars, was a prototype of the Messiah.

One day Jonathan decided to attack a whole garrison of the Philistines. The only one with him was a young man, a boy who carried his weaponry. He told the boy that he was going to attack the whole garrison, adding that it did not make any difference to the Lord whether it was many men or only a few who attacked the Philistines, who in the story represented the evil in the world.

The young man answered him: "Do all that your mind inclines to, I am with you. As your mind is, so is mine" (1 Sam 14:7). So Jonathan attacked, followed by the young man. Jonathan gave his enemies the mortal blow, and the boy followed him to help finish them off.

The story is rather gruesome, but it illustrates, though in a violent way, how we relate to what Jesus did in a non-violent way. Jesus did the main task; on the cross he overcame sin and evil. We have to continue to fulfill his messianic mission to the end. Filled with his Spirit, we are engaged in removing the remains of sin and evil.

This is the mission we are engaged in. Jesus will be with us until the task is completed. Let us not lose our contact with him, ever! Amen, Alleluia!

MY JOURNAL

MY JOURNAL

MY JOURNAL

MY JOURNAL

MY JOURNAL

MY JOURNAL

MY JOURNAL